BLACK LEGACY PRESS™
WWW.BLACKLEGACYPRESS.ORG

SLAVE NARRATIVES

VOLUME VIII
MARYLAND NARRATIVES

By
United States.
Work Projects Administration

ISBN: 978-1-63652-217-3

SLAVE NARRATIVES

A Folk History of Slavery in the United States.
From Interviews with Former Slaves

UNITED STATES.
WORK PROJECTS ADMINISTRATION

TYPEWRITTEN RECORDS PREPARED BY
THE FEDERAL WRITERS' PROJECT
1936-1938
ASSEMBLED BY
THE LIBRARY OF CONGRESS PROJECT
WORK PROJECTS ADMINISTRATION
FOR THE DISTRICT OF COLUMBIA
SPONSORED BY THE LIBRARY OF
CONGRESS

WASHINGTON 1941

VOLUME VIII
MARYLAND NARRATIVES

Prepared by
The Federal Writers' Project of
The Works Progress Administration
For the State of Maryland

CONTENTS

Maryland
[--]-23-37
Guthrie

AUNT LUCY [HW: BROOKS].
References: Interview with Aunt Lucy and her son, Lafayette
Brooks.

AUNT LUCY

Aunt Lucy, an ex-slave, lives with her son, Lafayette Brooks, in a shack on the Carroll Inn Springs
property at Forest Glen, Montgomery County,
Md.

To go to her home from Rockville, leave the Court
House going east on Montgomery Ave. and follow US
Highway No. 240, otherwise known as the Rockville Pike,
in its southeasterly direction, four and one half miles to
the junction with it on the left (east) of the Garrett Park
Road. This junction is directly opposite the entrance to
the Georgetown Preparatory School, which is on the west
of this road. Turn left on the Garrett Park Road and follow it through that place and crossing Rock Creek go to
Kensington. Here cross the tracks of the B.&O. R.R. and
parallel them onward to Forest Glen. From the railroad
station in this place go onward to Forest Glen. From the
railroad station in this place go onward on the same road
to the third lane branching off to the left. This lane will
be identified by the sign "Carroll Springs Inn". Turn left
here and enter the grounds of the inn. But do not go up in
front of the inn itself which is one quarter of a mile from

the road. Instead, where the drive swings to the right to go to the inn, bear to the left and continue downward fifty yards toward the swimming pool. Lucy's shack is on the left and one hundred feet west of the pool. It is about eleven miles from Rockville.

Lucy is an usual type of Negro and most probably is a descendant of less remotely removed African ancestors than the average plantation Negroes. She does not appear to be a mixed blood—a good guess would be that she is pure blooded Senegambian. She is tall and very thin, and considering her evident great age, very erect, her head is very broad, overhanging ears, her forehead broad and not so receeding as that of the average. Her eyes are wide apart and are bright and keen. She has no defect in hearing.

Following are some questions and her answers:

"Lucy, did you belong to the Carrolls before the war?" "Nosah, I didne lib around heah den. Ise born don on de bay".

"How old are you?"

"Dunno sah. Miss Anne, she had it written down in her book, but she said twas too much trouble for her to be always lookin it up". (Her son, Lafayette, says he was her eldest child and that he was born on the Severn River, in Maryland, the 15th day of October, 1872. Supposing the mother was twenty-five years old then, she would be about ninety now. Some think she is more than a hundred years old).

"Who did you belong to?"

"I belonged to Missus Ann Garner".

"Did she have many slaves?"

"Yassuh. She had seventy-five left she hadnt sold when the war ended".

"What kind of work did you have to do?"

"O, she would set me to pickin up feathers round de yaird. She had a powerful lot of geese. Den when I got a little bigger she had me set the table. I was just a little gal then. Missus used to say that she was going to make a nurse outen me. Said she was gwine to sen me to Baltimo to learn to be a nurse".

"And what did you think about that?"

"Oh; I thought that would be fine, but he war came befo I got big enough to learn to be a nurse".

"I remebers when the soldiers came. I think they were Yankee soldiers. De never hurt anybody but they took what they could find to eat and they made us cook for them. I remebers that me and some other lil gals had a play house, but when they came nigh I got skeered. I just ducked through a hole in the fence and ran out in the field. One of the soldiers seed me and he hollers 'look at that rat run'."

"I remebers when the Great Eastern (steamship which laid the Atlantic cable) came into the bay. Missus Ann, and all the white folks went down to Fairhaven wharf to see dat big shep".

"I stayed on de plantation awhile after de war and heped de Missus in de house. Den I went away".

"Ise had eight chillun. Dey all died and thisun and his brother (referring to Lafayette). Den his brother died too. I said he ought ter died instid o his brother."

"Why?"

"Because thisun got so skeered when he was little bein carried on a hos that he los his speech and de wouldt let me see im for two days. It was a long time befor he learned to talk again". (To this day he has such an impediment of speech that it is painful to hear him make the effort to talk).

"What did you have to eat down on the plantation, Aunt Lucy?"

"I hab mostly clabber, fish and corn bread. We gets plenty of fish down on de bay".

"When we cum up here we works in the ole Forest Glen hotel. Mistah Charley Keys owned the place then. We stayed there after Mr. Cassidy come. (Mr. Cassidy was the founder of the National Park Seminary, a school for girls). My son Lafayette worked there for thirty five years. Then we cum to Carroll Springs Inn".

Maryland
11/15/37
Rogers

CHARLES COLES, Ex-slave.
Reference: Personal interview with Charles Coles at his home,
1106 Sterling St., Baltimore, Md.

CHARLES COLES

"I was born near Pisgah, a small village in the western part of Charles County, about 1851. I do not know who my parents were nor my relatives. I was reared on a large farm owned by a man by the name of Silas Dorsey, a fine Christian gentleman and a member of the Catholic Church.

"Mr. Dorsey was a man of excellent reputation and character, was loved by all who knew him, black and white, especially his slaves. He was never known to be harsh or cruel to any of his slaves, of which he had more than 75.

"The slaves were Mr. Dorsey's family group, he and his wife were very considerate in all their dealings. In the winter the slaves wore good heavy clothes and shoes and in summer they were dressed in fine clothes.

"I have been told that the Dorseys' farm contained about 3500 acres, on which were 75 slaves. We had no overseers. Mr. and Mrs. Dorsey managed the farm. They required the farm hands to work from 7 A.M. to 6:00 P.M.; after that their time was their own.

"There were no jails nor was any whipping done on the farm. No one was bought or sold. Mr. and Mrs. Dorsey conducted regular religious services of the Catholic church on the farm in a chapel erected for that purpose and in which the slaves were taught the catechism and some learned how to read and write and were assisted by some Catholic priests who came to the farm on church holidays and on Sundays for that purpose. When a child was born, it was baptised by the priest, and given names and they were recorded in the Bible. We were taught the rituals of the Catholic church and when any one died, the funeral was conducted by a priest, the corpse was buried in the Dorseys' graveyard, a lot of about 1-1/2 acres, surrounded by cedar trees and well cared for. The only difference in the graves was that the Dorsey people had marble markers and the slaves had plain stones.

"I have never heard of any of the Dorseys' slaves running away. We did not have any trouble with the white people.

"The slaves lived in good quarters, each house was weather-boarded and stripped to keep out the cold. I do not remember whether the slaves worked or not on Saturdays, but I know the holidays were their own. Mr. Dorsey did not have dances and other kinds of antics that you expected to find on other plantations.

"We had many marbles and toys that poor children had, in that day my favorite game was marbles.

"When we took sick Mr. and Mrs. Dorsey had a doctor who admistered to the slaves, giving medical care that they needed. I am still a Catholic and will always be a member of St. Peter Clavier Church."

Maryland
Sept. 20, 1937
Rogers

JAMES V. DEANE, Ex-slave.
Reference: Personal interview with James V. Deane, ex-slave,
on Sept. 20, 1937, at his home, 1514 Druid Hill Ave.,
Baltimore.

JAMES V. DEANE

"I was born in a log cabin, a typical Charles County log cabin, at Goose Bay on the Potomac River. The plantation on which I was born fronted more than three miles on the river. The cabin had two rooms, one up and one down, very large with two windows, one in each room. There were no porches, over the door was a wide board to keep the rain and snow from beating over the top of the door, with a large log chimney on the outside, plastered between the logs, in which was a fireplace with an open grate to cook on and to put logs on the fire to heat.

"We slept on a home-made bedstead, on which was a straw mattress and upon that was a feather mattress, on which we used quilts made by my mother to cover.

"As a slave I worked on the farm with other small boys thinning corn, watching watermelon patches and later I worked in wheat and tobacco fields. The slaves never had nor earned any cash money.

"Our food was very plain, such as fat hog meat, fish

and vegetables raised on the farm and corn bread made up with salt and water.

"Yes, I have hunted o'possums, and coons. The last time I went coon hunting, we treed something. It fell out of the tree, everybody took to their heels, white and colored, the white men outran the colored hunter, leading the gang. I never went hunting afterwards.

"My choice food was fish and crabs cooked in all styles by mother. You have asked about gardens, yes, some slaves had small garden patches which they worked by moonlight.

"As for clothes, we all wore home-made clothes, the material woven on the looms in the clothes house. In the winter we had woolen clothes and in summer our clothes were made from cast-off clothes and Kentucky jeans. Our shoes were brogans with brass tips. On Sunday we fed the stock, after which we did what we wanted.

"I have seen many slave weddings, the master holding a broom handle, the groom jumping over it as a part of the wedding ceremony. When a slave married someone from another plantation, the master of the wife owned all the children. For the wedding the groom wore ordinary clothes, sometimes you could not tell the original outfit for the patches, and sometimes Kentucky jeans. The bride's trousseau, she would wear the cast-off clothes of the mistress, or, at other times the clothes made by other slaves.

"It was said our plantation contained 10,000 acres. We had a large number of slaves, I do not know the number. Our work was hard, from sunup to sundown. The slaves were not whipped.

"There was only one slave ever sold from the plantation, she was my aunt. The mistress slapped her one day, she struck her back. She was sold and taken south. We never saw or heard of her afterwards.

"We went to the white Methodist church with slave gallery, only white preachers. We sang with the white people. The Methodists were christened and the Baptists were baptised. I have seen many colored funerals with no service. A graveyard on the place, only a wooden post to show where you were buried.

"None of the slaves ran away. I have seen and heard many patrollers, but they never whipped any of Mason's slaves. The method of conveying news, you tell me and I tell you, but be careful, no troubles between whites and blacks.

"After work was done, the slaves would smoke, sing, tell ghost stories and tales, dances, music, home-made fiddles. Saturday was work day like any other day. We had all legal holidays. Christmas morning we went to the big house and got presents and had a big time all day.

"At corn shucking all the slaves from other plantations would come to the barn, the fiddler would sit on top of the highest barrel of corn, and play all kinds of songs, a barrel of cider, jug of whiskey, one man to dish out a drink of liquor each hour, cider when wanted. We had supper at twelve, roast pig for everybody, apple sauce, hominy, and corn bread. We went back to shucking. The carts from other farms would be there to haul it to the corn crib, dance would start after the corn was stored, we danced until daybreak.

"The only games we played were marbles, mumble pegs and ring plays. We sang London Bridge.

"When we wanted to meet at night we had an old conk, we blew that. We all would meet on the bank of the Potomac River and sing across the river to the slaves in Virginia, and they would sing back to us.

"Some people say there are no ghosts, but I saw one and I am satisfied, I saw an old lady who was dead, she was only five feet from me, I met her face to face. She was a white woman, I knew her. I liked to tore the door off the hinges getting away.

"My master's name was Thomas Mason, he was a man of weak mental disposition, his mother managed the affairs. He was kind. Mrs. Mason had a good disposition, she never permitted the slaves to be punished. The main house was very large with porches on three sides. No children, no overseer.

"The poor white people in Charles County were worse off than the slaves; because they could not get any work to do, on the plantation, the slaves did all the work.

"Some time ago you asked did I ever see slaves sold. I have seen slaves tied behind buggies going to Washington and some to Baltimore.

"No one was taught to read. We were taught the Lord's Prayer and catechism.

"When the slaves took sick Dr. Henry Mudd, the one who gave Booth first aid, was our doctor. The slaves had herbs of their own, and made their own salves. The only charms that were worn were made out of bones."

United States. Work Projects Administration

Maryland
11/3/37
Rogers

MRS. M.S. FAYMAN.
Reference: Personal interview with Mrs. Fayman,
at her home, Cherry Heights near Baltimore, Md.

MRS. M.S. FAYMAN

"I was born in St. Nazaire Parish in Louisiana, about 60 miles south of Baton Rouge, in 1850. My father and mother were Creoles, both of them were people of wealth and prestige in their day and considered very influential. My father's name was Henri de Sales and mother's maiden name, Marguerite Sanchez De Haryne. I had two brothers Henri and Jackson named after General Jackson, both of whom died quite young, leaving me the only living child. Both mother and father were born and reared in Louisiana. We lived in a large and spacious house surrounded by flowers and situated on a farm containing about 750 acres, on which we raised pelicans for sale in the market at New Orleans.

"When I was about 5 years old I was sent to a private School in Baton Rouge, conducted by French sisters, where I stayed until I was kidnapped in 1860. At that time I did not know how to speak English; French was the language spoken in my household and by the people in the parish.

"Baton Rouge, situated on the Mississippi, was a river

port and stopping place for all large river boats, especially between New Orleans and large towns and cities north. We children were taken out by the sisters after school and on Saturdays and holidays to walk. One of the places we went was the wharf. One day in June and on a Saturday a large boat was at the wharf going north on the Mississippi River. We children were there. Somehow, I was separated from the other children. I was taken up bodily by a white man, carried on the boat, put in a cabin and kept there until we got to Louisville, Kentucky, where I was taken off.

"After I arrived in Louisville I was taken to a farm near Frankfort and installed there virturally a slave until 1864, when I escaped through the kindness of a delightful Episcopalian woman from Cincinnati, Ohio. As I could not speak English, my chores were to act as a tutor and companion for the children of Pierce Buckran Haynes, a well known slave trader and plantation owner in Kentucky. Haynes wanted his children to speak French and it was my duty to teach them. I was the private companion of 3 girls and one small boy, each day I had to talk French and write French for them. They became very proficient in French and I in the rudiments of the English language.

"I slept in the children's quarters with the Haynes' children, ate and played with them. I had all the privileges of the household accorded me with the exception of one, I never was taken off nor permitted to leave the plantation. While on the plantation I wore good clothes, similar to those of the white children. Haynes was a merciless brutal tyrant with his slaves, punishing them severly and cruelly both by the lash and in the jail on the plantation.

"The name of the plantation where I was held as a

slave was called Beatrice Manor, after the wife of Haynes. It contained 8000 acres, of which more than 6000 acres were under cultivation, and having about 350 colored slaves and 5 or 6 overseers all of whom were white. The overseers were the overlords of the manor; as Haynes dealt extensively in tobacco and trading in slaves, he was away from the plantation nearly all the time. There was located on the top of the large tobacco warehouse a large bell, which was rung at sun up, twelve o'clock and at sundown, the year round. On the farm the slaves were assigned a task to do each day and In the event it was not finished they were severely whipped. While I never saw a slave whipped, I did see them afterwards, they were very badly marked and striped by the overseers who did the whipping.

"I have been back to the farm on several occasions, the first time in 1872 when I took my father there to show him the farm. At that time it was owned by Colonel Hawkins, a Confederate Army officer.

"Let me describe the huts, these buildings were built of stone, each one about 20 feet wide, 50 feet long, 9 feet high in the rear, about 12 feet high In front, with a slanting roof of chestnut boards and with a sliding door, two windows between each door back and front about 2x4 feet, at each end a door and window similar to those on the side. There were ten such buildings, to each building there was another building 12x15 feet, this was where the cooking was done. At each end of each building there was a fire place built and used for heating purposes. In front of each building there were barrels filled with water supplied by pipes from a large spring, situated about 300 yards on the side of a hill which was very rocky, where the stones were quarried to build the buildings on the farm. On the outside near each window and door there were iron rings firmly attached to the walls, through which an iron rod was inserted and locked each end every night, making it impossible for those inside to escape.

"There was one building used as a jail, built of stone about 20x40 feet with a hip roof about 25 feet high, 2-story. On the ground in each end was a fire place; in one end a small room, which was used as office; adjoining, there was another room where the whipping was done. To reach the second story there was built on the outside, steps leading to a door, through which the female prisoners were taken to the room. All of the buildings had dirt floors.

"I do not know much about the Negroes on the plantation who were there at that time. Slaves were brought and taken away always chained together, men walking and women in ox carts. I had heard of several escapes and many were captured. One of the overseers had a pack of 6 or 8 trained blood hounds which were used to trace escaping slaves.

"Before I close let me give you a sketch of my family tree. My grandmother was a Haitian Negress, grandfather a Frenchman. My father was a Creole.

"After returning home in 1864, I completed my high school education in New Orleans in 1870, graduated from Fisk University 1874, taught French there until 1883, married Prof. Payman, teacher of history and English. Since then I have lived in Washington, New York, and Louisianna. For further information, write me c/o Y.W.C.A. (col.), Baltimore, to be forwarded".

Maryland
Dec. 16, 1937
Rogers

THOMAS FOOTE'S STORY, A free Negro.
Reference: Personal interview with Thomas Foote,
at his home, Cockeysville, Md.

THOMAS FOOTE

" **M**y mother's name was Eliza Foote and my father's name was Thomas Foote. Father and mother of a large family that was reared on a small farm about a mile east of Cockeysville, a village situated on the Northern Central Railroad 15 miles north of Baltimore City.

"My mother's maiden name was Myers, a daughter of a free man of Baltimore County. In her younger days she was employed by Dr. Ensor, a homeopathic medical doctor of Cockeysville who was a noted doctor in his day. Mrs. Ensor, a very refined and cultured woman, taught her to read and write. My mother's duty along with her other work was to assist Dr. Ensor in the making of some of his medicine. In gaining practical experience and knowledge of different herbs and roots that Dr. Ensor used in the compounding of his medicine, used them for commercial purposes for herself among the slaves and free colored people of Baltimore County, especially of the Merrymans, Ridgelys, Roberts, Cockeys and May-fields. Her fame reached as far south as Baltimore City and north of Baltimore as far as the Pennsylvania line and the surrounding territory. She was styled and called the doctor woman both by the slaves and the free people. She was suspected by the white people but confided in by the colored people both for their ills and their troubles.

"My mother prescribed for her people and compounded medicine out of the same leaves, herbs and roots that Dr. Ensor did. Naturally her success along these lines was good. She also delivered many babies and acted as a midwife for the poor whites and the slaves and free Negroes of which there were a number in Baltimore County.

"The colored people have always been religiously inclined, believed in the power of prayer and whenever she attended anyone she always preceeded with a prayer. Mother told me and I have heard her tell others hundreds of times, that one time a slave of old man Cockey was seen coming from her home early in the morning. He had been there for treatment of an ailment which Dr. Ensor had failed to cure. After being treated by my mother for a time, he got well. When this slave was searched, he had in his possession a small bag in which a stone of a peculiar shape and several roots were found. He said that mother had given it to him, and it had the power over all with whom it came in contact.

"There were about this time a number of white people who had been going through Cockeysville, some trying to find out if there was any concerted move on the part of the slaves to run away, others contacting the free people to find out to what extent they had 'grape-vine' news of the action of the Negroes. The Negro who was seen coming from mother's home ran away. She was immediately accused of Voodooism by the whites of Cockeysville, she was taken to Towson jail, there confined and grilled by the sheriff of Baltimore County—the Cockeys, and several other men, all demanding that she tell where the escaped slave was. She knowing that the only way he could have escaped was by the York Road, north or south, the Northern Central Railroad or by the way of Deer Creek, a small creek east of Cockeysville. Both the York Road and the railroad were being watched, she logically thought that the only place was Deer Creek, so she told the sheriff to search Deer Creek. By accident he was found about eight miles up Deer Creek in a swamp with several other colored men who had run away.

"Mother was ordered to leave Baltimore County or to be sold into slavery. She went to York, Pennsylvania, where she stayed until 1865, when she returned to her home in Cockeysville; where a great many of her descendants live, now, on a hill that slopes west to Cockeysville Station, and is known as Foote's Hill by both white and colored people of Baltimore County today.

"I was born in Cockeysville in 1867, where I have lived since; reared a family of five children, three boys and two girls. I am a member of the A.M.E. Church at Cockeysville. I am a member of the Masonic Lodge and belong to Odd Fellows at Towson, Maryland. The Foote's descendants still own five or more homes at Cockeysville, and we are known from one end of the county to the other."

Maryland
Sept. 22, 1937
Rogers

MENELLIS GASSAWAY, Ex-slave.
Reference: Personal interview with Menellis Gassaway, ex-slave,
on Sept. 22, 1937, at M.E. Home, Carrollton Ave., Baltimore.

MENELLIS GASSAWAY

"My name is Menellis Gassaway, son of Owing and Annabel Gassaway. I was born in Freedom District, Carroll County, about 1850 or 52, brother of Henrietta, Menila and Villa. Our father and mother lived in Carroll County near Eldersberg in a stone and log cabin, consisting of two rooms, one up and one down, with four windows, two in each room, on a small farm situated on a public road, I don't know the name.

"My father worked on a small farm with no other slaves, but our family. We raised on the farm vegetables and grain, consisting of corn and wheat. Our farm produced wheat and corn, which was taken to the grist mill to be ground; besides, we raised hogs and a small number of other stock for food.

"During the time I was a slave and the short time it was, I can't remember what we wore or very much about local conditions. The people, that is the white people, were friendly with our family and other colored people so far as I can recall.

"I do not recall of seeing slaves sold nor did the man who owned our family buy or sell slaves. He was a small man.

"As to the farm, I do not know the size, but I know it was small. On the farm there was no jail, or punishment inflicted on Pap or Ma while they were there.

"There was no church on the farm, but we were members of the old side Methodist church, having a colored preacher. The church was a long ways from the farm.

"My father neglected his own education as well as his children. He could not read himself. He did not teach any of his children to read, of which we in later years saw the advantage.

"In Carroll County there were so many people who were Union men that it was dangerous for whites in some places to say they were Rebels. This made the colored and white people very friendly.

"Pap was given holidays when he wanted. I do not know whether he worked on Saturdays or not. On Sunday we went to church.

"My father was owned by a man by the name of Mr. Dorsey. My mother was bound out by Mr. Dorsey to a man by the name of Mr. Morris of Frederick County.

"I have never heard of many ghost stories. But I believe once, a conductor on the railroad train was killed and headed (beheaded), and after that, a ghost would appear on the spot where he was killed. Many people in the neighborhood saw him and people on the train often saw him when the train passed the spot where he was killed.

"So far as being sick, we did not have any doctors. The poor white could not afford to hire one, and the colored doctored themselves with herbs, teas and salves made by themselves."

United States. Work Projects Administration

Maryland
[--] 11, 1938
Rogers

CAROLINE HAMMOND, A fugitive.
Interview at her home, 4710 Falls Road, Baltimore, Md.

CAROLINE HAMMOND

"I was born in Anne Arundel County near Davidsonville about 3 miles from South River in the year 1844. The daughter of a free man and a slave woman, who was owned by Thomas Davidson, a slave owner and farmer of Anne Arundel. He had a large farm and about 25 slaves on his farm all of whom lived in small huts with the exception of several of the household help who ate and slept in the manor house. My mother being one of the household slaves, enjoyed certain privileges that the farm slaves did not. She was the head cook of Mr. Davidson's household.

"Mr. Davidson and his family were considered people of high social standing in Annapolis and the people in the county. Mr. Davidson entertained on a large scale, especially many of the officers of the Naval Academy at Annapolis and his friends from Baltimore. Mrs. Davidson's dishes were considered the finest, and to receive an invitation from the Davidsons meant that you would enjoy Maryland's finest terrapin and chicken besides the best wine and champagne on the market.

"All of the cooking was supervised by mother, and the

table was waited on by Uncle Billie, dressed in a uniform, decorated with brass buttons, braid and a fancy Test, his hands incased in white gloves. I can see him now, standing at the door, after he had rung the bell. When the family and guests came in he took his position behind Mr. Davidson ready to serve or to pass the plates, after they had been decorated with meats, fowl or whatever was to be eaten by the family or guest.

"Mr. Davidson was very good to his slaves, treating them with every consideration that he could, with the exception of freeing them; but Mrs. Davidson was hard on all the slaves, whenever she had the opportunity, driving them at full speed when working, giving different food of a coarser grade and not much of it. She was the daughter of one of the Revells of the county, a family whose reputation was known all over Maryland for their brutality with their slaves.

"Mother with the consent of Mr. Davidson, married George Berry, a free colored man of Annapolis with the proviso that he was to purchase mother within three years after marriage for $750 dollars and if any children were born they were to go with her. My father was a carpenter by trade, his services were much in demand. This gave him an opportunity to save money. Father often told me that he could save more than half of his income. He had plenty of work, doing repair and building, both for the white people and free colored people. Father paid Mr. Davidson for mother on the partial payment plan. He had paid up all but $40 on mother's account, when by accident Mr. Davidson was shot while ducking on the South River by one of the duck hunters, dying instantly.

"Mrs. Davidson assumed full control of the farm and

the slaves. When father wanted to pay off the balance due, $40.00, Mrs. Davidson refused to accept it, thus mother and I were to remain in slavery. Being a free man father had the privilege to go where he wanted to, provided he was endorsed by a white man who was known to the people and sheriffs, constables and officials of public conveyances. By bribery of the sheriff of Anne Arundel County father was given a passage to Baltimore for mother and me. On arriving in Baltimore, mother, father and I went to a white family on Ross Street—now Druid Hill Ave., where we were sheltered by the occupants, who were ardent supporters of the Underground Railroad.

"A reward of $50.00 each was offered for my father, mother and me, one by Mrs. Davidson and the other by the Sheriff of Anne Arundel County. At this time the Hookstown Road was one of the main turnpikes into Baltimore. A Mr. Coleman whose brother-in-law lived in Pennsylvania, used a large covered wagon to transport merchandise from Baltimore to different villages along the turnpike to Hanover, Pa., where he lived. Mother and father and I were concealed in a large wagon drawn, by six horses. On our way to Pennsylvania, we never alighted on the ground in any community or close to any settlement, fearful of being apprehended by people who were always looking for rewards.

"After arriving at Hanover, Pennsylvania, it was easy for us to get transportation farther north. They made their way to Scranton, Pennsylvania, in which place they both secured positions in the same family. Father and mother's salary combined was $27.50 per month. They stayed there until 1869. In the meantime I was being taught at a Quaker mission in Scranton. When we come to Baltimore

I entered the 7th grade grammar school in South Baltimore. After finishing the grammar school, I followed
cooking all my life before and after marriage. My husband James Berry, who waited at the Howard House, died
in 1927—aged 84. On my next birthday, which will occur
on the 22nd of November, I will be 95. I can see well, have
an excellent appetite, but my grandchildren will let me
eat only certain things that they say the doctor ordered
I should eat. On Christmas Day 49 children and grand-
children and some great-grandchildren gave me a Xmas
dinner and one hundred dollars for Xmas. I am happy
with all the comforts of a poor person not dependant on
any one else for tomorrow".

Maryland
Dec. 13, 1937
Rogers

PAGE HARRIS, Ex-slave.
Reference: Personal interview with Page Harris at his home,
Camp Parole, A.A.C. Co., Md.

PAGE HARRIS

"**I** was born in 1858 about 3 miles west of Chi-camuxen near the Potomac River in Charles County on the farm of Burton Stafford, better known as Blood Hound Manor. This name was applied because Mr. Stafford raised and trained blood hounds to track runaway slaves and to sell to slaveholders of Mary-land, Virginia and other southern states as far south as Mississippi and Louisiana.

"My father's name was Sam and mother's Mary, both of whom belonged to the Staffords and were reared in Charles County. They reared a family of nine children, I being the oldest and the only one born a slave, the rest free. I think it was in 1859 or it might be 1860 when the Staffords liberated my parents, not because he believed in the freedom of slaves but because of saving the lives of his entire family.

"Mrs. Stafford came from Prince William County, Vir-ginia, a county on the west side of the Potomac River in Virginia. Mr. and Mrs. Stafford had a large rowboat that they used on the Potomac as a fishing and oyster boat as well as a transportation boat across the Potomac River to Quantico, a small town in Prince William County, Va., and up Quantico Creek in the same county.

"I have been told by my parents and also by Joshua Stafford, the oldest son of Mr. Stafford, that one Sunday morning on the date as related in the story previously Mrs. Stafford and her 3 children were being rowed across the Potomac River to attend a Baptist church in Virginia of which she was a member. Suddenly a wind and a thunder storm arose causing the boat to capsize. My father was fishing from a log raft in the river, immediately went to their rescue. The wind blew the raft towards the centre of the stream and in line with the boat. He was able without assistance to save the whole family, diving into the river to rescue Mrs. Stafford after she had gone down. He pulled her on the raft and it was blown ashore with all aboard, but several miles down the stream. Everybody thought that the Staffords had been drowned as the boat floated to the shore, bottom upwards.

"As a reward Mr. Stafford took my father to the court house at La Plata, the county seat of Charles County, signed papers for the emancipation of him, my mother, and me, besides giving him money to help him to take his family to Philadelphia.

"I have a vague recollection of the Staffords' family, not enough to describe. They lived on a large farm situated in Charles County, a part bounding on the Potomac River and a cove that extends into the farm property. Much of the farm property was marshy and was suitable for the purpose of Mr. Stafford's living—raising and training blood hounds. I have been told by mother and father on many occasions that there were as many as a hundred dogs on the farm at times. Mr. Stafford had about 50 slaves on his farm. He had an original method in training young blood hounds, he would make one of the slaves traverse a course, at the end, the slave would climb a tree. The younger dogs led by an old dog, sometimes by several older dogs, would trail the slave until they reached the tree, then they would bark until taken away by the men who had charge of the dogs.

"Mr. Stafford's dogs were often sought to apprehend runaway slaves. He would charge according to the value and worth of the slave captured. His dogs were often taken to Virginia, sometimes to North Carolina, besides being used in Maryland. I have been told that when a slave was captured, besides the reward paid in money, that each dog was supposed to bite the slave to make him anxious to hunt human beings.

"There was a slaveholder in Charles County who had a very valuable slave, an expert carpenter and bricklayer, whose services were much sought after by the people in Southern Maryland. This slave could elude the best blood hounds in the State. It was always said that slaves, when they ran away, would try to go through a graveyard and if he or she could get dirt from the grave of some one that had been recently buried, sprinkle it behind them, the dogs could not follow the fleeing slave, and would howl and return home.

"Old Pete the mechanic was working on farm near La Plata, he decided to run away as he had done on several previous occasions. He was known by some as the herb doctor and healer. He would not be punished on any condition nor would he work unless he was paid something. It was said that he would save money and give it to people who wanted to run away. He was charged with aiding a girl to flee. He was to be whipped by the sheriff of Charles County for aiding the girl to run away. He heard of it, left the night before he was to be whipped, he went to the swamp in the cove or about 5 miles from where his master lived. He eluded the dogs for several weeks, escaped, got to Boston and no one to this day has any idea how he did it; but he did.

"In the year of 1866 my father returned to Maryland bringing with him mother and my brothers and sister. He selected Annapolis for his future home, where he secured work as a waiter at the Naval Academy, he continued there for more than 20 years. In the meantime after 1866 or 1868, when schools were opened for colored people, I went to a school that was established for colored children and taught by white teacher until I was about 17 years old, then I too worked at the Naval Academy waiting on the midshipmen. In those days you could make extra money, sometimes making more than your wages. About 1896 or '97 I purchased a farm near Camp Parole containing 120 acres, upon which I have lived since, raising a variety of vegetables for which Anne Arundel County is noted. I have been a member of Asbury Methodist Episcopal Church, Annapolis, for more than 40 years. All of my children, 5 in number, have grown to be men and women, one living home with me, one in New York, two in Baltimore, and one working in Washington, D.C."

Maryland
Sept. 27, 1937
Rogers

ANNIE YOUNG HENSON, Ex-slave.
Reference: Personal interview with Annie Young Henson, ex-slave,
at African M.E. Home, 207 Aisquith St., Baltimore.

ANNIE YOUNG HENSON

"I was born in Northumberland County, Virginia, 86 years ago. Daughter of Mina and Tom Miller. I had one brother Feelingchin and two sisters, Mary and Matilda. Owned by Doctor Pressley Nellum.

"The farm was called Traveler's Rest. The farm so named because a man once on a dark, cold and dreary night stopped there and asked for something to eat and lodging for the night; both of which was given and welcomed by the wayfarer.

"The house being very spacious with porches on each side, situated on a high hill, with trees on the lawn giving homes to the birds and shade to the master, mistress and their guests where they could hear the chant of the lark or the melodious voices of the slaves humming some familiar tunes that suited their taste, as they worked.

"Nearby was the slave quarters and the log cabin, where we lived, built about 25 feet from the other quarter. Our cabin was separate and distinct from the others. It contained two rooms, one up and one down, with a window in each room. This cabin was about 25 feet from the kitchen of the manor house, where the cooking was done by the kitchen help for the master, mistress and their guests, and from which each slave received his or her weekly ration, about 20 pounds of food each.

"The food consisted of beef, hog meat, and lamb or mutton and of the kind of vegetables that we raised on the farm.

"My position was second nurse for the doctor's family, or one of the inner servants of the family, not one of the field hands. In my position my clothes were made better, and better quality than the others, all made and arranged to suit the mistress' taste. I got a few things of femine dainty that was discarded by the mistress, but no money nor did I have any to spend. During my life as a slave I was whipped only once, and that was for a lie that was told on me by the first nurse who was jealous of my looks. I slept in the mistress' room in a bed that we pushed under the mistress' in the day or after I arose.

"Old Master had special dogs to hunt opossum, rabbit, coons and birds, and men to go with them on the hunt. When we seined, other slave owners would send some of their slaves to join ours and we then dividing the spoils of the catch.

"We had 60 slaves on the plantation, each family housed in a cabin built by the slaves for Nellums to accommodate the families according to the number. For clothes we had good clothes, as we raised sheep, we had our own wool, out of which we weaved our cloth, we called the cloth 'box and dice'.

"In the winter the field slaves would shell corn, cut

wood and thrash wheat and take care of the stock. We had our shoes made to order by the shoe maker.

"My mistress was not as well off before she married the doctor as afterward. I was small or young during my slave days, I always heard my mistress married for money and social condition. She would tell us how she used to say before she was married, when she saw the doctor coming, 'here comes old Dr. Nellums'. Another friend she would say 'here comes cozen Auckney'.

"We never had any overseers on the plantation, we had an old colored man by the name of Peter Taylor. His orders was law, if you wanted to please Mistress and Master, obey old Peter.

"The farm was very large, the slaves worked from sunup to sundown, no one was harshly treated or punished. They were punished only when proven guilty of crime charged.

"Our master never sold any slaves. We had a six-room house, where the slaves entertained and had them good times at nights and on holidays. We had no jail on the plantation. We were not taught to read or write, we were never told our age.

"We went to the white church on Sunday, up in the slave gallery where the slaves worshipped sometimes. The gallery was overcrowded with ours and slaves from other plantations. My mistress told me that there was once an old colored man who attended, taking his seat up in the gallery directly over the pulpit, he had the habit of saying Amen. A member of the church said to him, 'John, if you don't stop hollowing Amen you can't come to church'; he got so full of the Holy Ghost he yelled out Amen upon a venture, the congregation was so tickled with him and at his antics that they told him to come when and as often as he wanted.

"During my slave days only one slave ran away, he was my uncle, when the Yankees came to Virginia, he ran away with them. He was later captured by the sheriff and taken to the county jail. The Doctor went to the court house, after which we never heard nor saw my uncle afterwards.

"I have seen and heard white-cappers, they whipped several colored men of other plantations, just prior to the soldiers drilling to go to war.

"I remember well the day that Dr. Nellum, just as if it were yesterday, that we went to the court house to be set free. Dr. Nellum walked in front, 65 of us behind him. When we got there the sheriff asked him if they were his slaves. The Dr. said they were, but not now, after the papers were signed we all went back to the plantation. Some stayed there, others went away. I came to Baltimore and I have never been back since. I think I was about 17 or 18 years old when I came away. I worked for Mr. Marshall, a flour merchant, who lived on South Charles Street, getting $6.00 per month. I have been told by both white and colored people of Virginia who knew Dr. Nellum, he lost his mind."

Maryland
Sept. 29, 1937
Rogers

REV. SILAS JACKSON, Ex-slave.
Reference: Personal interview with Rev. Silas Jackson, ex-slave, at his home, 1630 N. Gilmor St., Baltimore.

REV. SILAS JACKSON

"I was born at or near Ashbie's Gap in Virginia, either in the year of 1846 or 47. I do not know which, but I will say I am 90 years of age. My father's name was Sling and mother's Sarah Louis. They were purchased by my master from a slave trader in Richmond, Virginia. My father was a man of large stature and my mother was tall and stately. They originally came from the Eastern Shore of Maryland, I think from the Legg estate, beyond that I do not know. I had three brothers and two sisters. My brothers older than I, and my sisters younger. Their names were Silas, Carter, Rap or Raymond, I do not remember; my sisters were Jane and Susie, both of whom are living in Virginia now. Only one I have ever seen and he came north with General Sherman, he died in 1925. He was a Baptist minister like myself.

"The only things I know about my grandparents were: My grandfather ran away through the aid of Harriet Tubman and went to Philadelphia and saved $350, and purchased my grandmother through the aid of a Quaker or an Episcopal minister, I do not know. I have on several occasions tried to trace this part of my family's past history, but without success.

"I was a large boy for my age, when I was nine years of age my task began and continued until 1864. You see I saw and I was a slave.

"In Virginia where I was, they raised tobacco, wheat, corn and farm products. I have had a taste of all the work on the farm, besides of digging and clearing up new ground to increase the acreage to the farm. We all had task work to do—men, women and boys. We began work on Monday and worked until Saturday. That day we were allowed to work for ourselves and to garden or to do extra work. When we could get work, or work on some one else's place, we got a pass from the overseer to go off the plantation, but to be back by nine o'clock on Saturday night or when cabin inspection was made. Some time we could earn as much as 50 cents a day, which we used to buy cakes, candies, or clothes.

"On Saturday each slave was given 10 pounds corn meal, a quart of black strap, 6 pounds of fat back, 3 pounds of flour and vegetables, all of which were raised on the farm. All of the slaves hunted or those who wanted, hunted rabbits, opossums or fished. These were our choice food as we did not get anything special from the overseer.

"Our food was cooked by our mothers or sisters and for those who were not married by the old women and men assigned for that work.

"Each family was given 3 acres to raise their chickens or vegetables and if a man raised his own food he was given $10.00 at Christmas time extra, besides his presents.

"In the summer or when warm weather came each slave was given something, the women, linsey goods or gingham clothes, the men overalls, muslin shirts, top and underclothes, two pair of shoes, and a straw hat to work in. In the cold weather, we wore woolen clothes, all made at the sewing cabin.

"My master was named Tom Ashbie, a meaner man was never born in Virginia—brutal, wicked and hard. He always carried a cowhide with him. If he saw anyone doing something that did not suit his taste, he would have the slave tied to a tree, man or woman, and then would cowhide the victim until he got tired, or sometimes, the slave would faint.

"The Ashbie's home was a large stone mansion, with a porch on three sides. Wide halls in the center up and down stairs, numerous rooms and a stone kitchen built on the back connected with dining room.

"Mrs. Ashbie was kind and lovely to her slaves when Mr. Ashbie was out. The Ashbies did not have any children of their own, but they had boys and girls of his own sister and they were much like him, they had maids or private waiter for the young men if they wanted them.

"I have heard it said by people in authority, Tom Ashbie owned 9000 acres of farm land besides of wood land. He was a large slave owner having more than 100 slaves on his farm. They were awakened by blowing of the horn before sunrise by the overseer, started work at sunrise and worked all day to sundown, with not time to go to the cabin for dinner, you carried your dinner with you. The slaves were driven at top speed and whipped at the snap of the finger, by the overseers, we had four overseers on the farm all hired white men.

"I have seen men beaten until they dropped in their tracks or knocked over by clubs, women stripped down to their waist and cowhided.

"I have heard it said that Tom Ashbie's father went to one of the cabins late at night, the slaves were having a secret prayer meeting. He heard one slave ask God to change the heart of his master and deliver him from slavery so that he may enjoy freedom. Before the next day the man disappeared, no one ever seeing him again; but after that down in the swamp at certain times of the moon, you could hear the man who prayed in the cabin praying. When old man Ashbie died, just before he died he told the white Baptist minister, that he had killed Zeek for praying and that he was going to hell.

"There was a stone building on the farm, it is there today. I saw it this summer while visiting in Virginia. The old jail, it is now used as a garage. Downstairs there were two rooms, one where some of the whipping was done, and the other used by the overseer. Upstairs was used for women and girls. The iron bars have coroded, but you can see where they were. I have never seen slaves sold on the farm, but I have seen them taken away, and brought there. Several times I have seen slaves chained taken away and chained when they came.

"No one on the place was taught to read or write. On Sunday the slaves who wanted to worship would gather at one of the large cabins with one of the overseers present and have their church. After which the overseer would talk. When communion was given the overseer was paid for staying there with half of the collection taken up, some time he would get 25¢. No one could read the Bible. Sandy Jasper, Mr. Ashbie's coachman was the preacher, he would go to the white Baptist church on Sunday with family and would be better informed because he heard the white preacher.

"Twice each year, after harvest and after New Year's, the slaves would have their protracted meeting or their revival and after each closing they would baptize in the creek, sometimes in the winter they would break the ice singing Going to the Water or some other hymn of that nature. And at each funeral, the Ashbies would attend the service conducted in the cabin there the deceased was, from there taken to the slave graveyard. A lot dedicated for that purpose, situated about 3/4 of a mile from cabins near a hill.

"There were a number of slaves on our plantation who ran away, some were captured and sold to a Georgia trader, others who were never captured. To intimidate the slaves, the overseers were connected with the patrollers, not only to watch our slaves, but sometimes for the rewards for other slaves who had run away from other plantations. This feature caused a great deal of trouble between the whites and blacks. In 1858 two white men were murdered near Warrenton on the road by colored people, it was never known whether by free people or slaves.

"When work was done the slaves retired to their cabins, some played games, others cooked or rested or did what they wanted. We did not work on Saturdays unless harvest times, then Saturdays were days of work. At other times, on Saturdays you were at leisure to do what you wanted. On Christmas day Mr. Ashbie would call all the slaves together, give them presents, money, after which they spent the day as they liked. On New Year's day we all were scared, that was the time for selling, buying and trading slaves. We did not know who was to go or come.

"I do not remember of playing any particular game, my sport was fishing. You see I do not believe in ghost stories nor voodooism, I have nothing to say. We boys used to take the horns of a dead cow or bull, cut the end off of it, we could blow it, some having different notes. We could tell who was blowing and from what plantation.

"When a slave took sick she or he would have to depend on herbs, salves or other remedies prepared by someone who knew the medicinal value. When a valuable hand took sick one of the overseers would go to Upper Ville for a doctor."

Maryland
[--]-20-37
Rogers

JAMES CALHART JAMES, Ex-slave.
Reference: Personal interview with James Calhart James, ex-slave, at his home, 2460 Druid Hill Ave., Baltimore.

JAMES CALHART JAMES

"My father's name was Franklin Pearce Randolph of Virginia, a descendant of the Randolphs of Virginia who migrated to South Carolina and located near Fort Sumter, the fort that was surrendered to the Confederates in 1851 or the beginning of the Civil War. My mother's name was Lottie Virginia James, daughter of an Indian and a slave woman, born on the Rapidan River in Virginia about 1823 or 24, I do not know which; she was a woman of fine features and very light in complexion with beautiful, long black hair. She was purchased by her master and taken to South Carolina when about 15 years old. She was the private maid of Mrs. Randolph until she died and then continued as housekeeper for her master, while there and in that capacity I was born on the Randolph's plantation August 23, 1846. I was a half brother to the children of the Randolphs, four in number. After I was born mother and I lived in the servants' quarters of the big house enjoying many pleasures that the other slaves did not: eating and sleeping in the big house, playing and associating with my half-brothers and sisters.

"As for my ancestors I have no recollection of them, the history of the Randolphs in Virginia is my background.

"My father told mother when I became of age, he was going to free me, send me north to be educated, but instead I was emancipated. During my slave days my father gave me money and good clothes to wear. I bought toys and games.

"My clothes were good both winter and summer and according to the weather.

"My master was my father; he was kind to me but hard on the field hands who worked in the rice fields. My mistress died before I was born. There were 3 girls and one boy, they treated me fairly good—at first or when I was small or until they realised their father was my father, then they hated me. We lived in a large white frame house containing about 15 rooms with every luxury of that day, my father being very rich.

"I have heard the Randolph plantation contained about 4000 acres and about 300 slaves. We had white overseers on the plantation, they worked hard producing rice on a very large scale, and late and early. I know they were severely punished, especially for not producing the amount of work assigned them or for things that the overseers thought they should be punished for.

"We had a jail over the rice barn where the slaves were confined, especially on Sundays, as punishment for things done during the week.

"I could read and write when I was 12 years old. I was taught by. the teacher who was the governess for the

44

Randolph children. Mother could also read and write. There was no church on the plantation; the slaves attended church on the next plantation, where the owner had a large slave church, he was a Baptist preacher, I attended the white church with the Randolph children. I was generally known and called Jim Randolph. I was baptised by the white Baptist minister and christened by a Methodist minister.

"There was little trouble between the white and blacks, you see I was one of the children of the house, I never came in contact much with other slaves. I was told that the slaves had a drink that was made of corn and rice which they drank. The overseers sometimes themselves drank it very freely. On holidays and Sundays the slaves had their times, and I never knew any difference as I was treated well by my father and did not associate with the other slaves.

"In the year of 1865, I left South Carolina, went to Washington, entered Howard University 1868, graduated in 1873, taught schools in Virginia, North Carolina and Maryland, retired 1910. Since then I have been connected with A.M.E. educational board. Now I am home with my granddaughter, a life well spent.

"One of the songs sung by the slaves on the plantation I can remember a part of it. They sang it with great feeling of happiness----

> Oh where shall we go when de great day comes
> An' de blowing of de trumpets and de bangins of de drums
> When General Sherman comes.

No more rice and cotton fields
We will hear no more crying
Old master will be sighing.

"I can't remember the tune, people sang it according to their own tune."

Slave Narratives

Maryland
Sept. 23, 1937
Rogers

MARY MORIAH ANNE SUSANNA JAMES, Ex-slave.
Reference: Personal interview with Mary James, ex-slave,
Sept. 23, 1937, at her home, 618 Haw St., Baltimore, Md.

MARY MORIAH ANNE SUSANNA JAMES

"My father's name was Caleb Harris James, and my mother's name was Mary Moriah. Both of them were owned by Silas Thornton Randorph, a distant relative of Patrick Henry. I have seen the picture of Patrick Henry many a time in the home place on the library wall. I had three sisters and two brothers. Two of my sisters were sold to a slave dealer from Georgia, one died in 1870. One brother ran away and the other joined the Union Army; he died in the Soldiers' Home in Washington in 1932 at the age of 84.

"How let me ask you, who told you about me? I knew that a stranger was coming, my nose has been itching for several days. How about my home life in Virginia, we lived on the James River in Virginia, on a farm containing more than 8,000 acres, fronting 3-1/2 miles on the river, with a landing where boats used to come to load tobacco and unload goods for the farm.

"The quarters where we lived on the plantation called

47

Randolph Manor were built like horse stables that you see on race tracks; they were 1-1/2 story high, about 25 feet wide, and about 75 feet long, with windows in the sides of the roofs. A long shelter on the front and at the rear. In front, people would have benches to sit on, and on the back were nails to hang pots and pans. Each family would have rooms according to the size of the family. There were 8 such houses, 6 for families and one for the girls and the other for the boys. In the quarters we had furniture made by the overseer and colored carpenters; they would make the tables, benches and beds for everybody. Our beds were ticking filled with straw and covers made of anything we could get.

"I have a faint recollection of my grandparents. My grandfather was sold to a man in South Carolina, to work in the rice field. Grandmother drowned herself in the river when she heard that grand-pap was going away. I was told that grandpap was sold because he got religious and prayed that God would set him and grandma free.

"When I was ten years old I was put to work on the farm with other children, picking weeds, stone up and tobacco worms and to do other work. We all got new shoes for Christmas, a dress and $2.50 for Christmas or suits of clothes. We spent our money at Mr. Randorph's store for things that we wanted, but was punished if the money was spent at the county seat at other stores.

"We were allowed fat meat, corn meal, black molasses and vegetables, corn and grain to roast for coffee. Mother cooked my food after stopping work on the farm for the day, I never ate possum. We would catch rabbits in guns or traps and as we lived on the rivers, we ate any kind of fish we caught. The men and everybody would go fishing after work. Each family had a garden, we raised what we wanted.

"As near as I can recall, we had about 150 sheep on the farm, producing our own wool. The old women weaved clothes; we had woolen clothes in the winter and cotton clothes in the summer. On Sunday we wore the clothes given to us at Christmas time and shoes likewise.

"I was married on the farm 1863 and married my same husband by a Baptist preacher in 1870 as I was told I had not been legally married. I was married in the dress given to me at Christmas of 1862. I did not get one in 1863.

"Old Silas Randolph was a mean man to his slaves, especially when drunk. He and the overseer would always be together, each of whom carried a whip, and upon the least provocation would whip his slaves. My mistress was not as mean as my master, but she was mean There was only one son in the Randolph family. He went to a military school somewhere in Virginia. I don't know the name. He was captured by the Union soldiers. I never saw him until after the war, when he came home with one arm.

"The overseer lived on the farm. He was the brother of Mrs. Randolph. He would whip men and women and children if he thought they were not working fast.

"The plantation house was a large brick house over-looking the river from a hill, a porch on three sides, two-stories and attic. In the attic slept the house servants and coachman. We did not come in contact with the white people very much. Our place was away from the village.

"There were 8,000 acres to the plantation, with more

than 150 slaves on it. I do not know the time slaves woke up, but everybody was at work at sunrise and worked to sundown. The slaves were whipped for not working fast or anything that suited the fancy of the master or overseer.

"I have seen slaves sold on the farm and I have seen slaves brought to the farm. The slaves were brought up the river in boats and unloaded at the landing, some crying and some seem to be happy.

"No one was taught to read or write. There was no church on the farm. No one was allowed to read the Bible or anything else.

"I have heard it said that the Randolph's lost more slaves by running away than anyone in the county. The patrollers were many in the county; they would whip any colored person caught off the place after night. Whenever a man wanted to run away he would go with someone else, either from the farm or from some other farm, hiding in the swamps or along the river, making their way to some place where they thought would be safe, sometimes hiding on trains leaving Virginia.

"The slaves, after going to their quarters, cooked, rested or did what they wanted. Saturdays was no different from Monday.

"On Christmas morning all the slaves would go up to the porch, get the $2.50, shoes and clothes, go back to the cabins and do what they wanted.

"On New Year's Day everybody was scared as that was the day that slaves were taken away or brought to the farm.

"You have asked about stories, I will tell you one I know. It is true.

"During the war one day some Union soldiers came to the farm looking for Rebels. There were a number of them in the woods near the landing; they had come across the river in boats. At night while the Union soldiers were at the landing, they were fired on by the Rebels. The Union soldiers went after them, killed ten, caught I think six and some were drowned in the river. Among the six was the overseer, and from that night people have heard shooting and seen soldiers. One night many years after the Civil War, while visiting a friend who now lives within 500 feet from the landing where the fighting took place, there appeared some soldiers carrying a man out of the woods whom I recognized as being the overseer. He had been seen hundreds of times by other people. White people will tell you the same thing. I will tell you for sure this is true.

"You must excuse me I wanted to see some friends this evening."

Maryland
9/14/37
Guthrie

PHILLIP JOHNSON, An Ex-Slave.
Ref: Phillip Johnson, R.F.D. Poolesville, Md.

PHILLIP JOHNSON

The subject of this sketch is a pure blooded Negro, whose kinky hair is now white, likewise his scraggy beard. He is of medium size and somewhat stooped with age, but still active enough to plant and tend a patch of corn and the chores about his little place at Sugarlands. His home is a small cabin with one or two rooms upstairs and three down, including the kitchen which is a leanto. The cabin is in great disrepair.

Phillip John is above the average in intelligence, has some education and is quite well versed in the Holy Scriptures, having been for many years a Methodist preacher among his people. He uses fairly good English and freely talks in answer to questions. Without giving the questions put to him by this writer, his remarks given in the first person and as near his own idiom are as follows:

"I'll be ninety years old next December. I dunno the day. My Missis had the colored folks ages written in a book but it was destroyed when the Confederate soldiers came through. But she had a son born two or three months younger than me and she remember that I was born in December, 1847, but she had forgot the day of the month.

"I was born down on the river bottom about four miles below Edwards' Ferry, on the Eight Mile Level, between Edwards' Ferry and Seneca. I belonged to ole Doctah White. He owned a lot o' lan down on de bottom. I dunno his first name. Everybody called him Doctah White. Yes, he was related to Doctah Elijah White. All the Whites in Montgomery County is related. Yes sah, Doctah White was good to his slaves. Yes sah, he had many slaves. I dunno how many. My Missis took me away from de bottom when I was a little boy, 'cause de overseer he was so cruel to me. Yes sah he was mean. I promised him a killin if ever I got big enough.

"We all liked the Missis. Everybody in dem days used to ride horseback. She would come ridin her horse down to de bottom with a great big basket of biscuits. We thought they were fine. We all glad to see de Missis a comin. We always had plenty to eat, such as it was. We had coarse food but there was plenty of it.

"The white folks made our clothes for us. They made linsey for the woman and woolen cloth for de men. They gave clothes sufficient to keep em warm. The men had wool clothes with brass buttons that had shanks on em. They looked good when they were new. They had better clothes then than most of us have now.

"They raised mostly corn an oats an wheat down on de river bottom in those days. They didn't raise tobacco. But I've heard say that they used to raise it long before I was born. They cut grain with cradles in dem days. They had a lot 'o men and would slay a lot 'o wheat in a day.

It was pretty work to see four or five cradlers in a field and others following them raking the wheat in bunches and others following binding them in bundles. The first reapers that came were called Dorsey reapers. They cut the grain and bunched it. It was then bound by hand.

"When my Missis took me away from the river bottom I lived in Poolesville where the Kohlhoss home and garage is. I worked around the house and garden. I remember when the Yankee and Confederate soldiers both came to Poolesville. Capn Sam White (son of the doctor) he join the Confederate in Virginia. He come home and say he goin to take me along back with him for to serve him. But the Yankees came and he left very sudden and leave me behind. I was glad I didn't have to go with him. I saw all that fightin around Poolesville. I used to like to watch em fightin. I saw a Yankee soldier shoot a Confederate and kill him. He raised his gun twice to shoot but he kept dodgin around the house an he didn' want to shoot when he might hit someone else. When he ran from the house he shot him.

"Yes sah, them Confederates done more things around here than the Yankees did. I remember once during the war they came to town. It was Sunday morning an I was sittin in the gallery of the ole brick Methodist church. One of them came to de door and he pointed his pistol right at that preacher's head. The gallery had an outside stairs then. I ran to de door to go down de stairs but there was another un there pointing his gun and they say don't nobody leave dis building. The others they was a cleanin up all the hosses and wagons round the church. The one who was guarding de stairs, he kept a lookin to see if dey was done cleaning up de hosses, and when he wasn't watching I slip half way down de stairs, an when he turn his back I jump down and run. When he looks he jus laugh.

"My father he lived to be eighty nine. He died right here in this house and he's buried over by the church. His name was Sam. They called my mother Willie Ann. She died when I was small. I had three brothers and one sister. My father married again and had seven or eight other children.

"I've had eleven children; five livin, six dead. I've been preaching for forty years and I have seen many souls saved. I don't preach regular anymore but once in a while I do. I have preached in all these little churches around here. I preached six years at Sugar Loaf Mountain. The presidin elder he wants me to go there. The man that had left there jus tore that church up. I went up there one Sunday and I didn't see anything that I could do. I think I'm not able for this. I said they needs a more experienced preacher than me. But the presidin elder keeps after me to go there and I says, well, I go for one year. Next thing it was the same thing. I stays on another year and so on for six years. When I left there that church was in pretty good shape.

"I think preaching the gospel is the greatest work in the world. But folks don't seem to take the interest in church that they used to."

Maryland
Sept. 30, 1937
Rogers

GEORGE JONES, Ex-slave.
Reference: Personal interview with George Jones, Ex-slave,
at African M.E. Home, 207 Aisquith St., Baltimore.

GEORGE JONES

"I was born in Frederick County, Maryland, 84 years ago or 1853. My father's name was Henry and mother's Jane; brothers Dave, Joe, Henry, John and sisters Annie and Josephine. I know my father and mother were slaves, but I do not recall to whom they belonged. I remember my grandparents.

"My father used to tell me how he would hide in the hay stacks at night, because he was whipped and treated badly by his master who was rough and hard-boiled on his slaves. Many a time the owner of the slaves and farm would come to the cabins late at night to catch the slaves in their dingy little hovels, which were constructed in cabin fashion and of stone and logs with their typical windows and rooms of one room up and one down with a window in each, the fireplaces built to heat and cook for occupants.

"The farm was like all other farms in Frederick County, raising grain, such as corn, wheat and fruit and on which work was seasonable, depending upon the weather, some seasons producing more and some less. When the season was good for the crop and crops plentiful, we had a little money as the plantation owner gave us some to spend.

"When hunting came, especially in the fall and winter, the weather was cold, I have often heard say father speak of rabbit, opossum and coon hunting and his dogs. You know in Frederick County there are plenty of woods, streams and places to hunt, giving homes and hiding places for such game.

"We dressed to meet the weather condition and wore shoes to suit rough traveling through woods and up and down the hills of the country.

"In my boyhood days, my father never spoke much of my master, only in the term I have expressed before, or the children, church, the poor white people in the neighborhood or the farm, their mode of living, social condition. I will say this in conclusion, the white people of Frederick County as a whole were kind towards the colored people and are today, very little race friction one way or the other."

Ellen B. Warfield
May 18, 1937

ALICE LEWIS.

ALICE LEWIS

Alice Lewis, ex-slave, 84, years old, in charge of sewing-room at Provident Hospital (Negro), Baltimore. Tall, slender, erect, her head crowned by abundant snow white wool, with a fine carriage and an air of poise mud self respect good to behold, Alice belies her 84 years.

"Yes'm, I was born in slavery, I don't look it, but I was! Way down in Wilkes County, Georgia, nigh to a little town named Washington which ain't so far from Augusta. My pappy, he belong to the Alexanders, and my mammy, she belong to the Wakefiel' plantation and we all live with the Wakefiel's. No ma'am, none of the Wakefiel' niggers ever run away. They was too well off! They knew who they friends was! My white folkses was good to their niggers! Them was the days when we had good food and it didn't cost nothing—chickens and hogs and garden truck. Saturdays was the day we got our 'lowance for the week, and lemme tell you, they didn't stint us none. The best in the land was what we had, jest what the white folkses had.

"Clothes? yes'm. We had two suits of clothes, a winter suit and a summer suit and two pairs of shoes, a winter pair and a summer pair. Yes'm, my mammy, she spin the cotton, yes'm picked right on the plantation, yes'm, cotton picking was fun, believe me! As I was saying, Mammy she spin and she wears the cloth, and she cut it out and she make our clothes. That's where I git my taste to sew, I reckon. When I first come to Baltimore, I done dressmaking, 'deed I did. I sewed for the best fam'lies in this yere town. I sewed for the Howards and the Slingluffs and the Jenkinses. Jest the other day, I met Miss C'milla down town and she say. 'Alice, ain' this you? and I say, 'Law me, Miss C'milla', and 'she say, 'Alice, why don' you come to see Mother? She ain' been so well—she love to see you....'

"Well, as I was a saying, we didn't work so hard, them days. We got up early, 'cause the fires had to be lighted to make the house warm for the white folks, but in them days, dinner was in the middle of the day—the quality had theirs at twelve o'clock—and they had a light supper at five and when we was through, we was through, and free to go the quarters and set around and smoke a pipe and rest.

"Yes'm they taught us to read and write. Sunday afternoons, my young mistresses used to teach the pickaninnies to read the Bible. Yes'm we was free to go to see the niggers on other plantations but we had to have a pass an' we was checked in an' out. No'm, I ain't never seen no slaves sold, nor none in chains, and I ain't never seen no Ku Kluxers.

"I live with the Wakefiel's till I was 'leven and then Marse Wakefiel' give me to my young mistress when she married and went to North Carolina to live. And 'twas in North Carolina that I seed Sherman, 'deed I did! I seed

Sherman and his sojers, gathering up all the hogs and all the hosses, and all the cows and all the little cullud chillen. Them was drefful days! These is drefful days, too. Old man Satan, he sure am on earth now.

"Yes'm, I believes in ghos'ses. I ain't never seed 'em but I is feel 'em. I live once in a house where a man was killed. I lie in my bed and they close in on me! No'm, I ain't afraid. The landlord say when I move out, 'you is stay there longer than anybody I ever had.' 'Nother house I live in (this was in North Carolina too), it had been a gamblin' house and it had hants. On rainy nights, I'd lie awake and hear "drip, drip ... drip, drip...." What was that? Why, that was the blood a dripping ... Why on rainy night? Why, on rainy nights, the blood gets a little fresh...!"

Maryland
Sept. 4, 1937
Rogers

PERRY LEWIS, Ex-slave.
Reference: Personal interview with Perry Lewis, ex-slave,
at his home, 1124 E. Lexington St., Baltimore.

PERRY LEWIS

" **I** was born on Kent Island, Md. about 86 years ago. My father's name was Henry and mother's Louise. I had one brother John, who was killed in the Civil War at the Deep Bottom, one sister as I can remember. My father was a freeman and my mother a slave, owned by Thomas Tolson, who owned a small farm on which I was born in a log cabin, with two rooms, one up and one down.

"As you know the mother was the owner of the children that she brought into the world. Mother being a slave made me a slave. She cooked and worked on the farm, ate whatever was in the farmhouse and did her share of work to keep and maintain the Tolsons. They being poor, not having a large place or a number of slaves to increase their wealth, made them little above the free colored people and with no knowledge, they could not teach me or any one else to read.

"You know the Eastern Shore of Maryland was in the most productive slave territory and where farming was done on a large scale; and in that part of Maryland where there were many poor people and many of whom were employed as overseers, you naturally heard of patrollers and we had them and many of them. I have heard that patrollers were on Kent Island and the colored people would go out in the country on the roads, create a disturbance to attract the patrollers' attention. They would tie ropes and grape vines across the roads, so when the patrollers would come to the scene of the disturbance on horseback and at full tilt, they would be throwing those who would come in contact with the rope or vine off the horse; sometimes badly injuring the riders. This would create hatred between the slaves, the free people, the patrollers and other white people who were concerned.

"In my childhood days I played marbles, this was the only game I remember playing. As I was on a small farm, we did not come in contact much with other children, and heard no children's songs. I therefore do not recall the songs we sang.

"I do not remember being sick but I have heard mother say, when she or her children were sick, the white doctor who attended the Tolsons treated us and the only herbs I can recall were life-everlasting boneset and woodditney, from each of which a tea could be made.

"This is about all I can recall."

Maryland
Sept. 7, 1937
Rogers

RICHARD MACKS, Ex-slave.
Reference: Personal interview with Richard Macks, ex-slave,
at his home, 541 W. Biddle St., Baltimore.

RICHARD MACKS

" I was born in Charles County in Southern Maryland in the year of 1844. My father's name was William (Bill) and Mother's Harriet Mack, both of whom were born and reared in Charles County—the county that James Wilkes Booth took refuge in after the assassination of President Lincoln in 1865. I had one sister named Jenny and no brothers: let me say right here it was God's blessing I did not. Near Bryantown, a county center prior to the Civil War as a market for tobacco, grain and market for slaves.

"In Bryantown there were several stores, two or three taverns or inns which were well known in their days for their hospitality to their guests and arrangements to house slaves. There were two inns both of which had long sheds, strongly built with cells downstairs for men and a large room above for women. At night the slave traders would bring their charges to the inns, pay for their meals, which were served on a long table in the shed, then afterwards, they were locked up for the night.

"I lived with my mother, father and sister in a log

cabin built of log and mud, having two rooms; one with a dirt floor and the other above, each room having two windows, but no glass. On a large farm or plantation owned by an old maid by the name of Sally McPherson on McPherson Farm.

"As a small boy and later on, until I was emancipated, I worked on the farm doing farm work, principally in the tobacco fields and in the woods cutting timber and firewood. I slept on a home-made bed or bunk, while my mother and sister slept in a bed made by father on which they had a mattress made by themselves and filled with straw, while dad slept on a bench beside the bed and that he used in the day as a work bench, mending shoes for the slaves and others. I have seen mother going to the fields each day like other slaves to do her part of the farming. I being considered as one of the household employees, my work was both in the field and around the stable, giving me an opportunity to meet people some of whom gave me a few pennies. By this method I earned some money which I gave to my mother. I once found a gold dollar, that was the first dollar I ever had in my life.

"We had nothing to eat but corn bread baked in ashes, fat back and vegetables raised on the farm; no ham or any other choice meats; and fish we caught out of the creeks and streams.

"My father had some very fine dogs; we hunted coons, rabbits and opossum. Our best dog was named Ruler, he would take your hat off. If my father said: 'Ruler, take his hat off!', he would jump up and grab your hat.

"We had a section of the farm that the slaves were allowed to farm for themselves, my mistress would let them raise extra food for their own use at nights. My father was the colored overseer, he had charge of the entire plantation and continued until he was too old to work, then mother's brother took it over, his name was Caleb.

"When I was a boy, I saw slaves going through and to Bryansville town. Some would be chained, some handcuffed, and others not. These slaves were bought up from time to time to be auctioned off or sold at Bryantown, to go to other farms, in Maryland, or shipped south.

"The slave traders would buy young and able farm men and well-developed young girls with fine physiques to barter and sell. They would bring them to the taverns where there would be the buyers and traders, display them and offer them for sale. At one of these gatherings a colored girl, a mulatto of fine stature and good looks, was put on sale. She was of high spirits and determined disposition. At night she was taken by the trader to his room to satisfy his bestial nature. She could not be coerced or forced by him [TR: 'by him' lined out] so she was attacked by him. In the struggle she grabbed a knife and with it, she sterilized[HW:?] him and from the result of injury he died the next day. She was charged with murder. Gen. Butler, hearing of it, sent troops to Charles County to protect her, they brought her to Baltimore, later she was taken to Washington where she was set free. She married a Government employe, reared a family of 3 children, one is a doctor practicing medicine in Baltimore and the other a retired school teacher, you know him well if I were to tell you who the doctor is. This attack was the result of being goodlooking, for which many a poor girl in Charles County paid the price. There are several cases I could mention, but they are distasteful to me.

"A certain slave would not permit this owner to whip him, who with overseer and several others overpowered the slave, tied him, put him across a hogshead and whipped him severely for three mornings in succession. Some one notified the magistrate at Bryantown of the brutality. He interfered in the treatment of this slave, threatening punishment. He was untied, he ran away, was caught by the constable, returned to his owner, melted sealing wax was poured over his back on the wounds inflicted by him, when whipping, the slave ran away again and never was caught.

"There was a doctor in the neighborhood who bought a girl and installed her on the place for his own use, his wife hearing of it severely beat her. One day her little child was playing in the yard. It fell head down in a post hole filled with water and drowned. His wife left him; afterward she said it was an affliction put on her husband for his sins.

"During hot weather we wore thin woolen clothes, the material being made on the farm from the wool of our sheep, in the winter we wore thicker clothes made on the farm by slaves, and for shoes our measures were taken of each slave with a stick, they were brought to Baltimore by the old mistress at the beginning of each season, if she or the one who did the measuring got the shoe too short or too small you had to wear it or go barefooted.

"We were never taught to read or write by white people.

"We had to go to the white church, sit in the rear, many times on the floor or stand up. We had a colored preacher, he would walk 10 miles, then walk back. I was not a member of church. We had no baptising, we were christened by the white preacher.

"We had a graveyard on the place. Whites were buried inside of railing and the slaves on the outside. The members of the white family had tombstones, the colored had headstones and cedar post to show where they were buried.

"In Charles County and in fact all of Southern Maryland tobacco was raised on a large scale. Men, women and children had to work hard to produce the required crops. The slaves did the work and they were driven at full speed sometimes by the owners and others by both owner and overseers. The slaves would run away from the farms whenever they had a chance, some were returned and others getting away. This made it very profitable to white men and constables to capture the runaways. This caused trouble between the colored people and whites, especially the free people, as some of them would be taken for slaves. I had heard of several killings resulting from fights at night.

"One time a slave ran away and was seen by a colored man, who was hunting, sitting on a log eating some food late in the night. He had a corn knife with him. When his master attempted to hit him with a whip, he retaliated with the knife, splitting the man's breast open, from which he died. The slave escaped and was never captured. The white cappers or patrollers in all of the counties of Southern Maryland scoured the swamps, rivers and fields without success.

"Let me explain to you very plain without prejudice one way or the other, I have had many opportunities, a chance to watch white men and women in my long career, colored women have many hard battles to fight to protect themselves from assault by employers, white male servants or by white men, many times not being able to protect, in fear of losing their positions. Then on the other hand they were subjected to many impositions by the women of the household through woman's jealousy.

"I remember well when President Buchanan was elected, I was a large boy. I came to Baltimore when General Grant was elected, worked in a livery stable for three years, three years with Dr. Owens as a waiter and coachman, 3 years with Mr. Thomas Winanson Baltimore Street as a butler, 3 years with Mr. Oscar Stillman of Boston, then 11 years with Mr. Robert Garrett on Mt. Vernon Place as head butler, after which I entered the catering business and continued until about twelve years ago. In my career I have had the opportunity to come in contact with the best white people and the most cultured class in Maryland and those visiting Baltimore. This class is about gone, now we have a new group, lacking the refinement, the culture and taste of those that have gone by.

"When I was a small boy I used to run races with other boys, play marbles and have jumping contests.

"At nights the slaves would go from one cabin to the other, talk, dance or play the fiddle or sing. Christmas everybody had holidays, our mistress never gave presents. Saturdays were half-day holidays unless planting and harvest times, then we worked all day.

"When the slaves took sick or some woman gave birth

to a child, herbs, salves, home liniments were used or a midwife or old mama was the attendant, unless severe sickness Miss McPherson would send for the white doctor, that was very seldom."

Maryland
Dec. 21, 1937
Rogers

TOM RANDALL, Ex-slave.
Reference: Personal interview with Tom Randall,
at his home, Oella, Md.

TOM RANDALL

"I was born in Ellicott City, Howard County, Maryland, in 1856, in a shack on a small street now known as New Cut Road—the name then, I do not know. My mother's name was Julia Bacon. Why my name was Randall I do not know, but possibly a man by the name of Randall was my father. I have never known nor seen my father. Mother was the cook at the Howard House; she was permitted to keep me with her. When I could remember things, I remember eating out of the skillets, pots and pans, after she had fried chicken, game or baked in them, always leaving something for me. When I grew larger and older I can recall how I used to carry wood in the kitchen, empty the rinds of potatoes, the leaves of cabbages and the leaves and tops of other plants.

"There was a colored man by the name of Joe Nick, called Old Nick by a great many white people of me city. Joe was owned by Rueben Rogers, a lawyer and farmer of Howard County. The farm was situated about 2-1/2 miles on a road that is the extension of Main Street, the leading street of Ellicott City. They never called me anything but

Tomy or Randy, other people told me that Thomas Randall, a merchant of Ellicott City, was my father.

"Mother was owned by a man by the name of O'Brien, a saloon or tavern keeper of the town. He conducted a saloon in Ellicott City for a long time until he became manager, or operator, of the Howard House of Ellicott City, a larger hotel and tavern in the city. Mother was a fine cook, especially of fowl and game. The Howard House was the gathering place of the formers, lawyers and business men of Howard and Frederick Counties and people of Baltimore who had business in the courts of Howard County and people of western Maryland on their way to Baltimore.

"Joe could read and write and was a good mechanic and wheelright. These accomplishments made him very valuable to Rogers' farm, as wagons, buggies, carriages, plows and other vehicles and tools had to be made and repaired.

"When I was about eight or nine years old Joe ran away, everybody saying to join the Union Army. Joe Nick drove a pair of horses, hitched to a covered wagon, to Ellicott City. The horses were found, but no Nick, Rogers offered a reward of $100.00 for the return of Nick. This offer drew to Ellicott City a number of people who had bloodhounds that were trained to hunt Negroes—some coming from Anne Arundel, Baltimore, Howard and counties of southern Maryland, each owner priding his pack as being the best pack in the town. They all stopped at the Howard House, naturally drinking, treating their friends and each other, they all discussed among themselves the reward and their packs of hounds, each one saying that his pack was the best. This boasting was backed by cash. Some cash, plus the reward on their hounds. In the meantime Old Joe was thinking, not boasting, but was riding the rail.

"Old Joe left Ellicott City on a freight train, going west, which he hopped when it was stalled on the Baltimore and Ohio railroad a short distance from the railroad station at Ellicott City. Old Joe could not leave on the passenger trains, as no Negro would be allowed on the trains unless he had a pass signed by his master or a free Negro, and had his papers.

"At dawn the hunters left the Howard House with the packs, accompanied by many friends and people who joined up for the sport of the chase. They went to Rogers' farm where the dogs were taken in packs to Nick's quarters so they could get the odor and scent of Nick. They had a twofold purpose, one to get the natural scent, the other was, if Old Nick had run away, he might come back at night to get some personal belongings, in that way the direction he had taken would be indicated by the scent and the hounds would soon track him down. The hounds were unleashed, each hunter going in a different direction without result. Then they circled the farm, some going 5 miles beyond the farm without result. After they had hunted all day they returned to the Howard House where they regaled themselves in pleasures of the hotel for the evening.

"In June of 1865 Old Nick returned to Ellicott City dressed in a uniform of blue, showing that he had joined the Federal Army. Mr. Rueben Rogers upon seeing him had him arrested, charging him with being a fugitive slave. He was confined in the jail there and held until the U.S. Marshal of Baltimore released him, arresting Rogers

and bringing him to Baltimore City where he was repri-
manded by the Federal Judge. This story is well known
by the older people of Howard County and traditionally
known by the younger generation of Ellicott City, and is
called 'Old Nick: Rogers' lemon.'"

Maryland
Sept. 28, 1937
Stansbury

DENNIS SIMMS, Ex-slave.
Reference: Personal interview with Dennis Simms, ex-slave,
September 19, 1937, at his home, 629 Mosher St., Baltimore.

DENNIS SIMMS

Born on a tobacco plantation at Contee, Prince Georges County, Maryland, June 17, 1841, Dennis Simms, Negro ex-slave, 628 Mosher Street, Baltimore, Maryland, is still working and expects to live to be a hundred years old.

He has one brother living, George Simms, of South River, Maryland, who was born July 18, 1849. Both of them were born on the Contee tobacco plantation, owned by Richard and Charles Contee, whose forbears were early settlers in the State.

Simms always carries a rabbit's foot, to which he attributes his good health and long life. He has been married four times since he gained his freedom. His fourth wife, Eliza Simms, 67 years old, is now in the Providence Hospital, suffering from a broken hip she received in a fall. The aged Negro recalls many interesting and exciting incidents of slavery days. More than a hundred slaves worked on the plantation, some continuing to work for the Contee brothers when they were set free. It was a pretty hard and cruel life for the darkeys, declares the Negro.

Describing the general conditions of Maryland slaves, he said: "We would work from sunrise to sunset every day except Sundays and on New Year's Day. Christmas made little difference at Contee, except that we were given extra rations of food then. We had to toe the mark or be flogged with a rawhide whip, and almost every day there was from two to ten thrashings given on the plantations to disobedient Negro slaves.

"When we behaved we were not whipped, but the overseer kept a pretty close eye on us. We all hated what they called the 'nine ninety-nine', usually a flogging until fell over unconscious or begged for mercy. We stuck pretty close to the cabins after dark, for if we were caught roaming about we would be unmercifully whipped. If a slave was caught beyond the limits of the plantation where he was employed, without the company of a white person or without written permit of his master, any person who apprehended him was permitted to give him 20 lashes across the bare back.

"If a slave went on another plantation without a written permit from his master, on lawful business, the owner of the plantation would usually give the offender 10 lashes. We were never allowed to congregate after work, never went to church, and could not read or write for we were kept in ignorance. We were very unhappy.

"Sometimes Negro slave runaways who were apprehended by the patrollers, who kept a constant watch for escaped slaves, besides being flogged, would be branded with a hot iron on the cheek with the letter 'R'." Simms claimed he knew two slaves so branded.

Simms asserted that even as late as 1856 the Constitution of Maryland enacted that a Negro convicted of murder should have his right hand cut off, should be hanged in the usual manner, the head severed from the body, divided into four quarters and set up in the most public places of the county where the act was committed. He said that the slaves pretty well knew about this barbarous Maryland law, and that he even heard of dismemberments for atrocious crimes of Negroes in Maryland.

"We lived in rudely constructed log houses, one story in heighth, with huge stone chimneys, and slept on beds of straw. Slaves were pretty tired after their long day's work in the field. Sometimes we would, unbeknown to our master, assemble in a cabin and sing songs and spirituals. Our favorite spirituals were—Bringin' in de sheaves, De Stars am shinin' for us all, Hear de Angels callin', and The Debil has no place here. The singing was usually to the accompaniment of a Jew's harp and fiddle, or banjo. In summer the slaves went without shoes and wore three-quarter checkered baggy pants, some wearing only a long shirt to cover their body. We wore ox-hide shoes, much too large. In winter time the shoes were stuffed with paper to keep out the cold. We called them 'Program' shoes. We had no money to spend, in fact did not know the value of money.

"Our food consisted of bread, hominy, black strap molasses and a red herring a day. Sometimes, by special permission from our master or overseer, we would go hunting and catch a coon or possum and a pot pie would be a real treat.

"We all thought of running off to Canada or to Washington, but feared the patrollers. As a rule most slaves were lazy."

Simms' work at Contee was to saddle the horses, cut wood, and make fires and sometimes work in the field.

He voted for President Lincoln and witnessed the second inauguration of Lincoln after he was set free.

Maryland
12/6/37
Rogers

JIM TAYLOR (UNCLE JIM), Ex-slave.
Reference: Personal interview with Jim Taylor,
at his home, 424 E. 23rd St., Baltimore.

JIM TAYLOR

"I was born in Talbot County, Eastern Shore, Maryland, near St. Michaels about 1847. Mr. Mason Shehan's father knew me well as I worked for him for more than 30 years after the emancipation. My mother and father both were owned by a Mr. Davis of St. Michaels who had several tugs and small boats. In the summer, the small boats were used to haul produce while the tugs were used for towing coal and lumber on the Chesapeake Bay and the small rivers on the Eastern Shore. Mr. Davis bought able-bodied colored men for service on the boats. They were sail boats. I would say about 50 or 60 feet long. On each boat, besides the Captain, there were from 6 to 10 men used. On the tugs there were more men, besides the mess boy, than on the sail boats.

"I think a man by the name of Robinson who was in the coal business at Havre de Grace engaged Mr. Davis to tow several barges of soft coal to St. Michaels. It was on July 4th when we arrived at Havre de Grace. Being a holiday, we had to wait until the 5th, before we could start towards St. Michaels.

"Mr. Tuttle, the captain of the tug, did not sleep on the boat that night, but went to a cock fight. The colored men decided to escape and go to Pennsylvania. (I was a small boy). They ran the tug across the bay to Elk Creek, and upon arriving there they beached the tug on the north side, followed a stream that Harriett Tubman had told them about. After traveling about seven miles, they approached a house situated on a large farm which was occupied by one of the deputy sheriffs of the county. The sheriff told them they were under arrest. One of the escaping man seized the sheriff from the rear, after he was thrown they tied him, then they continued on a road towards Pennsylvania. They reached Pennsylvania about dawn. After they had gone some distance in Pennsylvania three men with guns overtook them; but five men and one woman of Pennsylvania with guns and clubs stopped them. In the meantime the sheriff and two of his deputies come up. The sheriff said he had to hold them for the authorities of the county. They were taken by the sheriff from the three men, carried about 15 miles further in Pennsylvania and then were told to go to Chester where they would be safe.

"Mr. Davis came to Chester with Mr. Tuttle to claim the escaping slaves. They were badly beaten, Mr. Tuttle receiving a fractured skull. There were several white men in Chester who were very much interested in colored people, they gave us money to go to Philadelphia. After arriving in Philadelphia, we went to Allen's mission, a colored church that helped escaping slaves. I stayed in Philadelphia until I was about 19 years old, then all the colored people were free. I returned to Talbot, there remained until 1904, came to Baltimore where I secured a job with James Hitchens, a colored man, who had six furniture vans drawn by two horses each and sometimes by three and four horses. Mr. Hitchens' office and warehouse were on North Street near Pleasant. I stayed there with Mr. Hitchens until he sold his business to Mr. O. Farror after he had taken sick.

"In March I will be 90 years old. I have been sick three times in my life. I am, and have been a member of North Street Baptist Church for thirty-three years. I am the father of nine children, have been married twice and a grandfather of twenty-three granddaughters and grandsons and forty-five great grand-children.

"While in Philadelphia I attended free school for colored children conducted at Allen's Mission; when I returned to Talbot county I was in the sixth grade or the sixth reader. Since then I have always been fond of reading. My favored books are the Bible, Bunyan's Pilgrim's Progress, Uncle Tom's Cabin, the lives of Napoleon, Frederick Douglass and Booker T. Washington, and church magazines and the Afro-American."

Maryland
[--]-22-37
Rogers

JAMES WIGGINS, Ex-slave.
Reference: Personal interview with James Wiggins, ex-slave,
at his home, 625 Barre St.

JAMES WIGGINS

"I was born in Anne Arundel County, on a farm near West River about 1850 or 1851, I do not know which. I do not know my father or mother. Peter Brooks, one of the oldest colored men in the county, told me that my father's name was Wiggins. He said that he was one of the Revells' slaves. He acquired my father at an auction sale held in Baltimore at a high price from a trader who had an office on Pratt Street about 1845. He was given a wife by Mr. Revell and as a result of this union I was born. My father was a carpenter by trade, he was hired out to different farmers by Mr. Revell to repair and build barns, fences and houses. I have been told that my father could read and write. Once he was charged with writing passes for some slaves in the county, as a result of this he was given 15 lashes by the sheriff of the county, immediately afterwards he ran away, went to Philadelphia, where he died while working to save money to purchase mother's freedom, through a white Baptist minister in Baltimore.

"I was called "Gingerbread" by the Revells. They reared me until I reached the age of about nine or ten years old. My duty was to put logs on the fireplaces in the Revells' house and work around the house. I remember well when I was taken to Annapolis, how I used to dance in the stores for men and women, they would give me pennies and three cent pieces, all of which was given to me by the Revells. They bought me shoes and clothes with the money collected.

"Mr. Revell died in 1861 or 62. The sheriff and men came from Annapolis, sold the slaves, stock and other chattels. I was purchased by a Mr. Mayland, who kept a store in Annapolis. I was sold by him to a slave trader to be shipped to Georgia. I was brought to Baltimore, and was jailed in a small house on Paca near Lombard. The trader was buying other slaves to make a load. I escaped through the aid of a German shoemaker, who sold shoes to owners for slaves.

"The German shoeman had a covered wagon, I was put in the wagon covered by boxes, taken to a house on South Sharp Street and there kept until a Mr. George Stone took me to Frederick City where I stayed until 1863, when Mr. Stone, a member of the Lutheran church, had me christened giving me the name of James Wiggins. This is how I got the name of Wiggins, after my father, instead of Gingerbread, through the investigation and the information given by Mr. Brooks.

"You know the Revells are well known in Anne Arundel County, consisting of a large family, each family a large property owner. I can't say how many acres were owned by Jim Revell, he was a general farmer having a few slaves, you see I was a small boy. I can't answer all the questions you want.

"There were a great many people in Anne Arundel who did not believe in slavery and many free colored people. These conditions caused conflicts between the free colored who many times were charged with aiding the slaves and the whites who were not favorably impressed with slavery and the others who believed in slavery. As a result, the patrollers were numerous. I remember of seeing Jim Revell coming home very much battered and beaten up as a result of an encounter with a number of free people and white people and those who were members of the patrollers.

"As a child I was very fond of dancing, especially the jig and buck. I made money as I stated before, I played children's plays of that time, top, marbles and another game we called skinny. Skinny was a game played on trees and grape vines.

"As a boy I was very healthy, I never had a doctor until I was over 50 years old. I don't know anything about the medical treatment of that day, you never need medicine unless you are ailing and I never ailed."

Maryland
Sept. 27, 1937
Stansbury

"PARSON" REZIN WILLIAMS, ex-slave.

References:
Baltimore Morning Sun, December 10, 1928.
Registration Books of Board of Election Supervisors
Baltimore Court House.

Personal interviews with "Parson" Rezin Williams,
on Thursday afternoon, September 18 and 24, 1937,
at his home, 2610 Pierpont Street, Mount Winans,
Baltimore, Md.

Maryland Historical Magazine, Vol 1 (1906), p. 56.

Buchholz: Governors of Maryland—pp. 57-63, 192-167.
(P.L.G. 28 B 92.)

REZIN WILLIAMS

"Parson" Williams----

Oldest living Negro Civil War veteran; now 116 years old.

Oldest registered voter in Maryland and said to be the oldest
"freeman" in the United States.

Said to be oldest member of Negro family in America with sister
and brother still living, more than a century old.

Father worked for George Washington.

In 1864 when the State Constitution abolished slavery and freed about 83,000 Negro slaves in Maryland, there was one, "Parson" Rezin Williams, already a freeman. He is now living at the age of 116 years, in Baltimore City, Maryland, credited with being the oldest of his race in the United States who served in the Civil War.

He was born March 11, 1822, at "Fairview", near Bowie, Prince Georges County, Maryland—a plantation of 1000 acres, then belonging to Governor Oden Bowie's father. "Parson" Williams' father, Rezin Williams, a freeman, was born at "Mattaponi", near Nottingham, Prince Georges County, the estate of Robert Bowie of Revolutionary War fame, friend of Washington and twice Governor of Maryland. The elder Rezin Williams served the father of our country as a hostler at Mount Vernon, where he worked on Washington's plantation during the stormy days of the Revolution.

There is perhaps nowhere to be found a more picturesque and interesting character of the colored race than "Parson" Williams, who, besides serving as a colored bishop of the Union American Methodist Church (colored) for more than a half century, is the composer of Negro spirituals which were popular during their day. He attended President Lincoln's inauguration and subsequently every Republican and Democratic presidential inauguration, although he himself is a Republican. Lincoln, according to Williams, shook hands with him in Washington.

One of Williams' sons, of a family of fourteen children, was named after George Washington, and another after Abraham Lincoln. The son, George Washington Williams, died in 1912 at the age of seventy-three years.

"Parson" Williams, serving the Union forces as a teamster, hauled munitions and supplies for General Grant's army, at Gettysburg. On trips to the rear, he conveyed wounded soldiers from the line of fire. He also served under General McClellan and General Hooker.

Although now confined to his home with infirmities of age, he posesses all his faculties and has a good memory of events since his boyhood days. Due to the fact that his grandmother was an Indian the daughter of an Indian chieftan, alleged to be buried in a vault in Baltimore County, Williams was a freeman like his father and hired himself out.

Williams claims that his father, when a boy, accompanied Robert Bowie, for whom he was working, to Mount Vernon, where he first met George Washington. He said that General Washington once became very angry at his father because he struck an unruly horse, exclaiming: "The brute has more sense than some slaves. Cease striking the animal."

Robert Bowie, the third son of Capt. William and Margaret (Sprigg) Bowie, was born at "Mattaponi", near Nottingham, March 1750. As a captain of a company of militia organized at Nottingham, he accompanied the Maryland forces when they joined Washington in his early campaign near New York. He and Washington became friends. In 1791, when Captain William Bowie died, his son Robert inherited "Mattaponi". He was the first

Democratic governor to be elected, one of the presidential electors for Madison, and a director of the first bank established at Annapolis.

Williams recalls hearing his father say that when Washington died, December 14, 1799, many paid reverence by wearing mourning scarfs and hatbands.

He recalls many interesting incidents during slavery days. He said that slaves could not buy or sell anything except with the permission of their master. If a slave was caught ten miles from his master's home, and had no signed permit, he was arrested as a runaway and harshly punished.

There was a standing reward for the capture of a runaway. The Indians who caught a runaway slave received a "match coat." The master gave the slave usually ten to ninety-nine lashes for running off. What slaves feared most was what they called the "nine ninety-nine" or 99 lashes with a rawhide whip, and sometimes they were unmercifully flogged until unconcious. Some cruel masters believed Negroes had no souls. The slaves at Bowie, however, declared "Parson" Williams, were pretty well treated and usually respected the overseers. He said that the slaves at Bowie mostly lived in cabins made of slabs running up and down and crudely furnished. Working time was from sunrise until sunset. The slaves had no money to spend and few masters allowed them to indulge in a religious meeting or even learn about the Bible.

Slaves received medical attention from a physician if they were seriously ill. When a death occured, a rough box would be made of heavy slabs and the dead Negro buried the same day on the plantation burying lot with a brief ceremony, if any. The grieving darkeys, relatives, after he was "eased" in the ground, would sing a few spirituals and return to their cabins.

Familiar old spirituals were composed by "Parson" Williams, including Roll De Stones Away, You'll Rise in De Skies, and Ezekiel, He'se Comin Home.

Following is one of Williams' spirituals:

> When dat are ole chariot comes,
> I'm gwine to lebe you:
> I'm bound for de promised land
> I'm gwine to lebe you.
>
> I'm sorry I'm gwine to lebe you,
> Farewell, oh farewell
> But I'll meet you in de mornin
> Farewell, oh farewell.

Still another favorite of "Parson" Williams, which he composed on Col. Bowie's plantation just before the Civil War, a sort of rallying song expressing what Canada meant to the slaves at that time, runs thus:

> I'm now embarked for yonder shore
> There a man's a man by law;
> The iron horse will bear me o'er
> To shake de lion's paw.
> Oh, righteous Father, will thou not pity me
> And aid me on to Canada, where all the
> slaves are free.
>
> Oh, I heard Queen Victoria say
> That if we would forsake our native land of

slavery,
And come across de lake
That she was standin' on de shore
Wid arms extended wide,
To give us all a peaceful home
Beyond de rollin' tide.

Interesting reminiscences are recalled by "Parson" Williams of his early life. He said that he still remembers when Mr. Oden Bowie (later governor) left with the army of invasion of Mexico (1846-1848), and of his being brought home ill after several years was nursed back to health at "Fairview". Governor Bowie died on his plantation in 1894 and is buried in the family burying ground there.

He was the first president of the Maryland Jockey Club. Governor Bowie raised a long string of famous race horses that became known throughout the country. From the "Fairview" stables went such celebrated horses as Dickens, Catespy, Crickmore, Commensation, Creknob, who carried the Bowie colors to the front on many well-contested race courses. After Governor Bowie's death, the estate became the property of his youngest son, W. Booth Bowie.

"Fairview" is located in the upper part of what was called the "Forest" of Prince Georges County, a few miles southwest of Collington Station. It is a fine type of old Colonial mansion built of brick, the place having been in the posession of the family for some time previous. "Fairview" is one of the oldest and finest homes in Maryland. The mansion contains a wide hall and is a typical Southern home.

Baruch Duckett married Kitty Bean, a granddaughter of John Bowie, Sr., the first of his name to come to Prince Georges County. They had but one daughter, whose name was Kitty Bean Duckett, and she married in 1800 William Bowie of Walter. Baruch Duckett outlived his wife and died in 1810. He devised "Fairview" to his son-in-law and the latter's children, and it ultimately became the property of his grandson, afterward known as Col. William B.[TR.?] Bowie, who made it his home until 1880, when he gave it to his eldest son, Oden, who in 1868 became Governor of Maryland. Governor Bowie was always identified with the Democratic Party.

"Parson" Williams' wife, Amelia Addison Williams died August 9, 1928, at the age of 94 years. The aged negro is the father of 14 children, one still living,—Mrs. Amelia Besley, 67 years old, 2010 Pierpont Street, Mount Winans, Baltimore, Maryland. His brother, Marcellus Williams, and a single sister, Amelia Williams, both living, reside on Rubio street, Philidelphia, Pa. According to "Parson" Williams, they are both more than a century old and are in fairly good health. Besides his children and a brother and a sister, Williams has several grandchildren, great-grandchildren and great-great-grandchildren living.

President Lincoln, Williams says, was looked upon by many slaves as a messenger from heaven. Of course, many slave masters were kind and considerate, but to most slaves they were just a driver and the slaves were work horses for them. Only once during his lifetime does Williams recall tasting whisky, when his cousin bought a pint. It cost three cents in those days. He said his mother used to make beer out of persimmons and cornhusks, but they don't make it any more, so he doesn't even drink beer now. He would much rather have a good cigar. He has since a boy, smoked a pipe.

By special permission of plantation owners in Prince Georges, St. Marys, Baltimore and other counties in Maryland, he was often permitted to visit the darkeys and conduct a religious meeting in their cabins. He usually wore a long-tailed black "Kentucky" suit with baggy trousers and sported a cane.

Usually when servants or slaves in those days found themselves happy and contented, it was because they were born under a lucky star. As for eating, they seldom got chicken, mostly they ate red herring and molasses— they called black strap molasses. They were allowed a herring a day as part of their food. Slaves as a rule preferred possums to rabbits. Some liked fish best. Williams' favorite food was cornpone and fried liver.

"Once before de wah, I was ridin Lazy, my donkey, a few miles from de boss' place at Fairview, when along came a dozen or more patrollers. Dey questioned me and decided I was a runaway slave and dey wuz gwine to give me a coat of tar and feathers when de boss rode up and ordered my release. He told dem dreaded white patrollers dat I was a freeman and a 'parson'."

When the slaves were made free, some of the overseers tooted horns, calling the blacks from their toil in the fields. They were told they need no longer work for their masters unless they so desired. Most of the darkeys quit "den and dar" and made a quick departure to other parts, but some remained and to this day their descendants are still to be found working on the original plantations, but of course for pay.

Describing the clothing worn in summer time by the slaves, he said they mostly went barefooted. The men and boys wore homespun, three-quarter striped pants and sometimes a large funnel-shaped straw hat. Some wore only a shirt as a covering for their body.

"In winter oxhide shoes were worn, much too large, and the soles contained several layers of paper. We called them 'program' shoes, because the paper used for stuffing, consisted of discarded programs. We gathered herbs from which we made medicine, snake root and sassafras bark being a great remedy for many ailments."

Williams, though himself not a slave by virtue of the fact that his grandmother was an Indian, was considered a good judge of healthy slaves, those who would prove profitable to their owners, so he often accompanied slave purchasers to the Baltimore slave markets.

He told of having been taken by a certain slave master to the Baltimore wharf, boarded a boat and after the slave dealer and the captain negotiated a deal, he, Williams, not realizing that he was being used as a decoy, led a group of some thirty or forty blacks, men, women and children, through a dark and dirty tunnel for a distance of several blocks to a slave market pen, where they were placed on the auction block.

He was told to sort of pacify the black women who set up a wail when they were separated from their husbands and children. It was a pitiful sight to see them, half naked, some whipped into submission, cast into slave pens surrounded by iron bars. A good healthy negro man from 18 to 30 would bring from $200 to $800. Women would bring about half the price of the men. Often when the women parted with their children and loved ones, they would never see them again.

Such conditions as existed in the Baltimore slave markets, which were considered the most important in the country, and the subsequent ill treatment of the unfortunates, hastened the war between the states.

The increasing numbers of free negroes also had much to do with causing the civil war. The South was finding black slavery a sort of white elephant. Everywhere the question was what to do with the freeman. Nobody wanted them. Some states declared they were a public nuisance.

"Uncle Rezin", by which name some called him, since slavery days, was, besides being engaged in preaching the Gospel, journeying from one town to another, where he has performed hundreds of marriages among his race, baptised thousands, performed numerous christenings and probably preached more sermons than any Negro now living. He preached his last sermon two years ago. He says his life's work is now through and he is crossing over the River Jordan and will soon be on the other side. Since the Civil War he has made extra money for his support during depression times by doing odd jobs of whitewashing, serving as a porter or janitor, cutting wood, hauling and running errands, also serving as a teamster, picking berries and working as a laborer. He has had several miraculous escapes from death during his long life. Twice during the past quarter of a century his home at Mount Winans has been destroyed by fire, when firemen rescued him in the nick of time, and some years ago, when he was suddenly awakened during a severe windstorm, his house was unroofed and blew down. When workmen were clearing away the debris in search for "Uncle" Rezin, some hours later, a voice was heard coming from a large barrel in the cellar. It was from Williams, who somehow managed to crawl in the barrel during the storm, and called out: "De Lord hab sabed me. You all haul me out of here, but I'se all right." Scabo, his pet dog, was killed by the falling debris during the storm. Firemen at Westport state that three years ago, when fire damaged "Uncle" Rezin's home, the aged negro preacher refused to be rescued, and walked out of the building through stifling smoke, as though nothing had happened. When veterans of a great war have been mowed down by the scythe of Father Time until their numbers are few, an added public interest attaches to them. Baltimore septuagenarians remember the honor paid to the last surviving "Old Defenders", who faced the British troops at North Point in 1814, and now the few veterans of the War of Secession, whether they wore the blue or the gray, receive similar attention. A far different class, one peculiarly associated with the strife between the North and the South, are approaching the point of fading out from the life of today—the old slaves, and original old freemen. "Parson" Williams tops the list of them all.

www.ingramcontent.com/pod-product-compliance
Lightning Source LLC
LaVergne TN
LVHW021537080426
835509LV00019B/2698